21 Affirmations for the Naturalistah

Ms. Folasayo

Dedication and Acknowledgments

Writing is a form of expression and healing for me. I thank God for turning my pain into gain. He is taking me from glory to glory through sharing my story. My prayer is that everyone who reads my book has a testimony of great self-image. May every reader see themselves the way God does. I would also like to thank my parents, family, friends, and mentors for their support.

It's Time

Hey lady in the mirror.
I want to take care of you.
I will take care of you.
All of you.
From the crown of your head to the
soles of your feet.
I don't care about the weather, the
elements, or the past.
My love is here.
Here to last.
Here to heal you from the inside out.
So stop hiding in the mirror.
It's time to come out.
It's time.

Introduction

Throughout my life I struggled with my hair. It was hard to manage. I felt so much pain when I combed it. To make matters worse my hair wasn't straight. As I grew into a young lady I realized my hair is beautiful just the way it is. I wrote these affirmations to encourage and inspire you.

CONTENTS

1 CARING AND NUTURING AFFIRMATIONS

1.) I am patient, gentle, and easy going with my hair.

Narrative

I learned that my hair responds well to gentleness and patience. This allows my hair to be thoroughly clean, detangled, and styled. All of such led to length retention.

Below write your own affirmation, thoughts, and questions.

_____

_____

_____

_____

_____

_____

_____

_____

2.) Taking care of my hair is opening doors to take care of myself inside out.

Narrative

There is a lot of factual information about hair out there. I learned that a head full of healthy hair starts inside the body. My outside appearance is a reflection of my inside appearance. This led to self-care, cherishing my temple, self-love, and wellness.

Below write your own affirmation,
thoughts, and questions.

_____

_____

_____

_____

_____

_____

_____

_____

3.) This hair of mine is like a plant. I water my plant.

Narrative

Natural hair can be very dry because of its tight curl pattern. When it rains plants are sustained. When natural hair is moisturized it is sustained.

Below write your own affirmation, thoughts, and questions.

_____

_____

_____

_____

_____

_____

_____

_____

4.) My hands are nurturing hands.
Every touch is a touch of nurture.

Narrative

As a mother nurtures her child I
nurture my hair. It is as simple as that.

Below write your own affirmation, thoughts, and questions.

_____

_____

_____

_____

_____

_____

_____

_____

5.) I have hair loving hands. They are mine. All mine. Mine for my mane.

Narrative

You ever see those old school movies with ladies wearing afros? They're patting their afros and shaping their fros. Well. . . oh what would I do without my hair loving hands?

Below write your own affirmation, thoughts, and questions.

_____

_____

_____

_____

_____

_____

_____

_____

2 STYLING AND PRODUCT AFFIRMATIONS

1.) A bun, ponytail, braids, twists, rain, snow, or shine. No matter the style. No matter the weather. My hair will shine.

Narrative

Natural Hair is so versatile. Sometimes my hair doesn't quite come out right. But I choose to work it.

Below write your own affirmation, thoughts, and questions.

_____

_____

_____

_____

_____

_____

_____

_____

2.) The ends of my hair embrace
the moisture of jojoba oil.

Narrative

The ends of hair is the most
vulnerable to breakage. It needs
moisture regularly. My ends respond
well to oiling it very lightly every other
day.

Below write your own affirmation, thoughts, and questions.

_____

_____

_____

_____

_____

_____

_____

_____

3.) One step at a time. One big chop, new style, and silk scarf at a time. One step at a time.

Narrative

Being natural for is me is a journey. I've learned what works for me through trial and error. I take it one step at a time(a lesson I can apply to every aspect of life).

Below write your own affirmation, thoughts, and questions.

_____

_____

_____

_____

_____

_____

_____

_____

4.) I'm natural and sometimes I still sleep pretty.

Narrative

This has always made me laugh. I thought those days were over. But oh no no no. Sometimes I want a certain style and sleeping pretty is a must.

Below write your own affirmation,
thoughts, and questions.

_____

_____

_____

_____

_____

_____

_____

_____

5.) A little bit of this. A little bit of that and I get all that. All that Shea butter mix cuz I'm all that. All that. I'm all that.

Narrative

I believe every woman should have her own home made hair cream. I started mixing my own Shea butter cream. This is a reflection of how in tune I'm in with what works for me.

Below write your own affirmation, thoughts, and questions.

_____

_____

_____

_____

_____

_____

_____

_____

6.) My two strand twists are neck turning twists. Don't look and drive while you tryna catch an eye of my two strand twists. My two strand twists.

Narrative

Throughout my natural hair journey I've seen how great two strand twists look on me. I've also felt people's eyes on my hair a lot. So I chuckle in appreciation. I also hope they're paying attention to the road or what they're doing.

Below write your own affirmation, thoughts, and questions.

_____

_____

_____

_____

_____

_____

_____

_____

7.) Saturdays are the best days. No
work. No school. Just the peace
and tranquility of my conditioning
cap and I.

Narrative

There is something so therapeutic
about washdays. Washing and
conditioning my hair is so soothing.
Both help me relax and mellow out.

Below write your own affirmation, thoughts, and questions.

_____

_____

_____

_____

_____

_____

_____

8.) My beloved Shea butter is like water in the desert. Shea butter brings the best out of my glory.

Narrative

Words cannot do enough to describe how special Shea Butter is to me. It brings out my true curl pattern. I even enjoy its earthy smell.

Below write your own affirmation,
thoughts, and questions.

_____

_____

_____

_____

_____

_____

_____

_____

9.) I work hard and smart. I treat myself to a deep condition every wash day. I deserve and enjoy it.

Narrative

This is the least I can do. This is my way of enjoying and appreciating myself. I deserve it and you do too.

Below write your own affirmation,
thoughts, and questions.

_____

_____

_____

_____

_____

_____

_____

_____

10.) Each braid, cornrow, twist, bantu knot, and flat twist is an act of self-love, self-embrace, and self-care.

Narrative

I really take my time when I do my hair. Each touch is one of care. I am graceful with my hair. My hair is receptive to gracefulness.

Below write your own affirmation, thoughts, and questions.

_____

_____

_____

_____

_____

_____

_____

_____

11.) I focus on the good hair days and improve the bad ones.

Narrative

Focusing on the good hair days makes me feel like a queen. After all I am a queen. I end up having more good hair days this way.

Below write your own affirmation, thoughts, and questions.

_____

_____

_____

_____

_____

_____

_____

_____

3 POSITIVE PERSPICTIVE AFFIRMATIONS

1.) Being different is a blessing. My hair is different.
Therefore my hair is a blessing.

Narrative

I really love my curl pattern. I'm in love with its tightness. I enjoy trying to run my hands through my hair. My hands might get stuck. It does take effort to run my hands through my hair. That's kind of cool to me.

Below write your own affirmation,
thoughts, and questions.

_____

_____

_____

_____

_____

_____

_____

2.) My hair is my crown of glory. Fearfully and wonderfully made is my crown of glory.

Narrative

I see my hair as being a gift from God. Not only that, but it is on top of my head. What a glorious gift. I therefore call my hair Glory. I am also royalty because I belong to God. Every queen wears a crown. Just as God made me in his image he crowned me Glory(anyone who has been bullied should read this daily).

Below write your own affirmation, thoughts, and questions.

_____

_____

_____

_____

_____

_____

_____

_____

3.) My crown of glory tells a story, a story of a journey.

Narrative

My coils have endured much. I haven't always cherished my coils. But still my coils have endured. I stand united with my hair. This union is permanent. To reach this great place has been a journey and will continue to be.

Below write your own affirmation, thoughts, and questions.

_____

_____

_____

_____

_____

_____

_____

4.) Confidence is contagious.
When I embrace my hair others
do too.

Narrative

When I first started college(I went to
Morgan State University. Go Bears!)
so many colleagues of mine were
impressed by my hair. So were my
friends and family. Today many of
them are natural. I consider myself a
trailblazer. You never know who is
watching you. You never know who
you inspire.

Below write your own affirmation, thoughts, and questions.

_____

_____

_____

_____

_____

_____

_____

5.) I am an afro sister and I affirm my afro. I am therefore an AffirmFroTiCulturlist.

Narrative

Natural hair has returned from the seventies political statement to a millennial movement. There are still barriers to overcome from corporate America all the way to personal relationships. It takes love of self to embrace one's true self. When you need encouragement look in the mirror and speak of your beauty. That is how you affirm your afro sistah. For more encouragement join the "AffirmFroTiCulture" group on Facebook.

Below write your own affirmation, thoughts, and questions.

_____

_____

_____

_____

_____

_____

_____

Conclusion

It has been a great pleasure narrating powerful affirmations. I hope you have been encouraged. I hope you have discovered your hair is beautiful. Be affirmed my Afro sistah.

Inside Out

I am learning to think well of my hair.
I am starting today.
I am starting now.
I am worthy and I embrace my crown
of glory.
Starting today.
Starting now.
I am healing from the inside out.
Amen

About the Author

Folasayo Onireti is a natural hair beautician and artist. She goes by Ms. Folasayo. Ms. Folasayo resides in her home Prince Georges County, Maryland. Morgan State University is where she earned her Bachelors of Science in Accounting. Accounting is a tool to advance career and endeavors she pursues. Ms. Folasayo has chosen to do what she does well effortlessly. She is endowed in the creative realm. Everything she touches from poetry to hair is blessed. Her natural hair is her joy. When she was sixteen years old she began caring for her own hair. Since then she has fully embraced her hair. Now Ms. Folasayo inspires other women to do the same through AffirmFroTiCulture. She is the Founder, CEO, and AffirmFroTiCulturlist- a woman who encourages the cultivation of natural hair. She is the middle of three children and loves to keep her head in the middle of a book. Getting lost in a good book is fun to her. That is why she wrote her book *21 Affirmations for the Naturalistah.* She loves the serenity that comes with nature. Rain calms her soul while plants and butterflies warm her heart. Her prayer is that the words of her book have the same impact on her readers.

Did you enjoy this book? Do you have questions? Did this book impact your life? Would you like to work with me?

Please contact me at:

iammsfolasayo@gmail.com

Notes

_____

_____

_____

_____

_____

_____

_____

_____

_____

_____

_____

_____

_____

_____

_____

_____

_____

21 Affirmations for the Naturalistah

_____

_____

_____

_____

_____

_____

_____

_____

_____

_____

_____

_____

_____

_____

_____

Made in the USA
Lexington, KY
02 March 2018